THE GLOW·IN·THE·DARK NIGHT SKY BOOK

By Clint Hatchett
Illustrated by Stephen Marchesi

RANDOM HOUSE 🏠 NEW YORK

FOR THOUSANDS OF YEARS, people have looked up at the sky and wondered about it. To help them make sense of what they saw, people of long ago played a game. They drew lines between the stars, filled in the rest with their imagination, and created constellations—pictures in the sky of people, animals, and other things.

To early cultures, this "game" was also a serious business. People needed to be familiar with the stars because the constellations, which move around the sky during the year, told them when the seasons would change. From this they knew when to plant and harvest their crops and when to start preparing for the cold, short days of winter. Early people also used the stars to find their way on the open sea. Long ago in the South Pacific, for example, sailors followed the stars and guided their boats from one tiny island to another until they populated an area larger than the United States.

Many of the constellations in this book were named long ago by the early Greeks, Romans, and Babylonians. These ancient people honored the heroes—and villains—of many of their favorite stories by placing them in the sky. You can read about some of these stories on the last page of this book.

HOW TO USE THIS BOOK

The star maps in this book will glow in the dark after you expose them to light. Outside, you'll be able to find more than thirty constellations in the night sky because the shining stars on the maps will show you what they look like. All you'll need is a flashlight to "recharge" the maps.

The maps are divided by season, so before you go outside, first turn to the right map. Then look at the time chart next to the map. It will tell you roughly what time, in each month, the position of the constellations on the map will match their position in the sky. (The times shown on the charts reflect daylight savings time beginning on the first Sunday in April and ending on the last Sunday in October. If the dates for daylight savings are different in your area, the stars in the sky will be in a slightly different position from the map at that time of night.)

On each two-page spread, one map shows illustrations of the constellations as the creatures the ancients imagined long ago. The other map shows simple diagrams of these constellations. The stars that form each constellation—plus Polaris, the North Star—will glow in the dark.

To use the star maps, you need to know where south is. If you're not sure, look at the map and find the Big Dipper (part of Ursa Major, the Great Bear; in spring), the Summer Triangle (a group of three bright stars from three different constellations; in summer and fall), or Orion the Hunter (in winter). One of these three star groupings appears on every map. Carefully study the grouping you've chosen; you can use it to find your bearings outside.

While you're still indoors, hold your map up to a bright light for a few minutes to make the stars glow. Now grab your flashlight and go outside.

When you're outside, look in the sky and find the star grouping you've chosen. Then turn the map until the position of the stars on the map matches their position in the sky. From the map, you should then be able to figure out which way is south on your horizon.

Face south, and turn the map so that south is at the bottom. Then raise the map over your head and compare the glowing patterns there with those in the sky. (If the stars on the map stop glowing, just shine the flashlight on them for a few minutes.)

Can you find Polaris (the North Star) in the tail of Ursa Minor (the Little Bear, also known as the Little Dipper)? Do you see the wide-spread wings of Cygnus the Swan? With a little practice, you'll soon be able to find all of the constellations in this book and join the ancient sky-watchers in their fascination with the stars—both indoors and out!

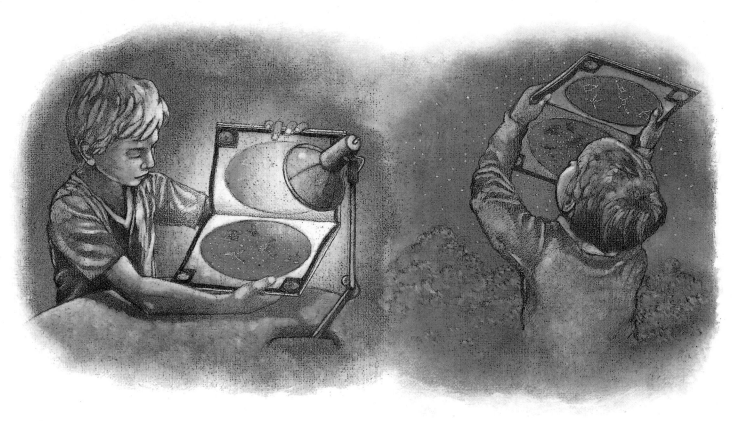

FULL MOON

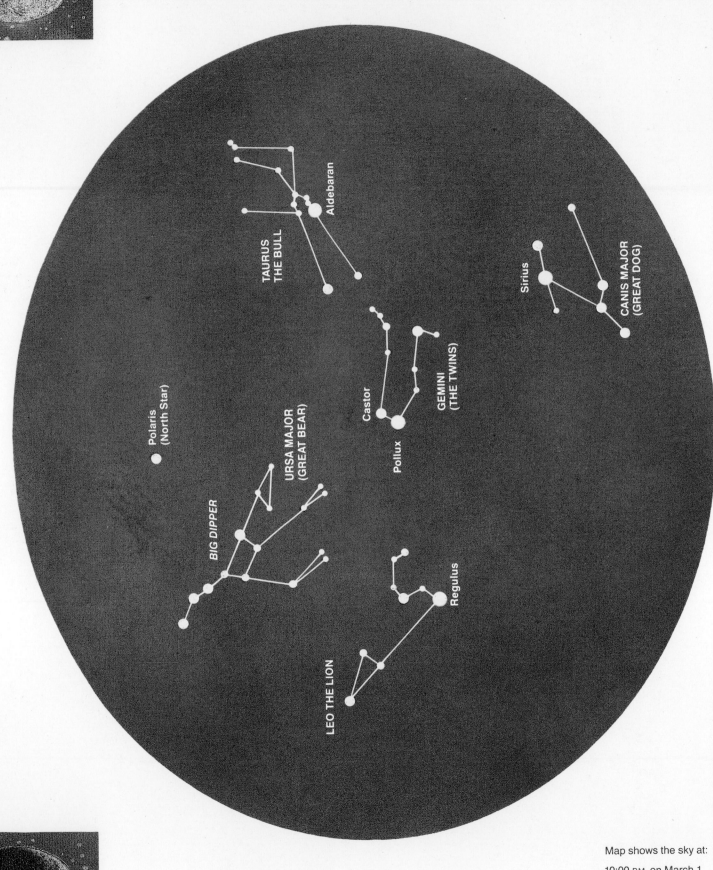

TAURUS
THE BULL

Aldebaran

Sirius

CANIS MAJOR
(GREAT DOG)

Castor

GEMINI
(THE TWINS)

Polaris
(North Star)

Pollux

URSA MAJOR
(GREAT BEAR)

BIG DIPPER

Regulus

LEO THE LION

CRESCENT MOON

Map shows the sky at:

10:00 P.M. on March 1
9:00 P.M. on March 15
8:00 P.M. on April 1
8:00 P.M. on April 15
7:00 P.M. on May 1

EARLY SPRING

GIBBOUS MOON

FIRST-QUARTER
MOON

EARTH

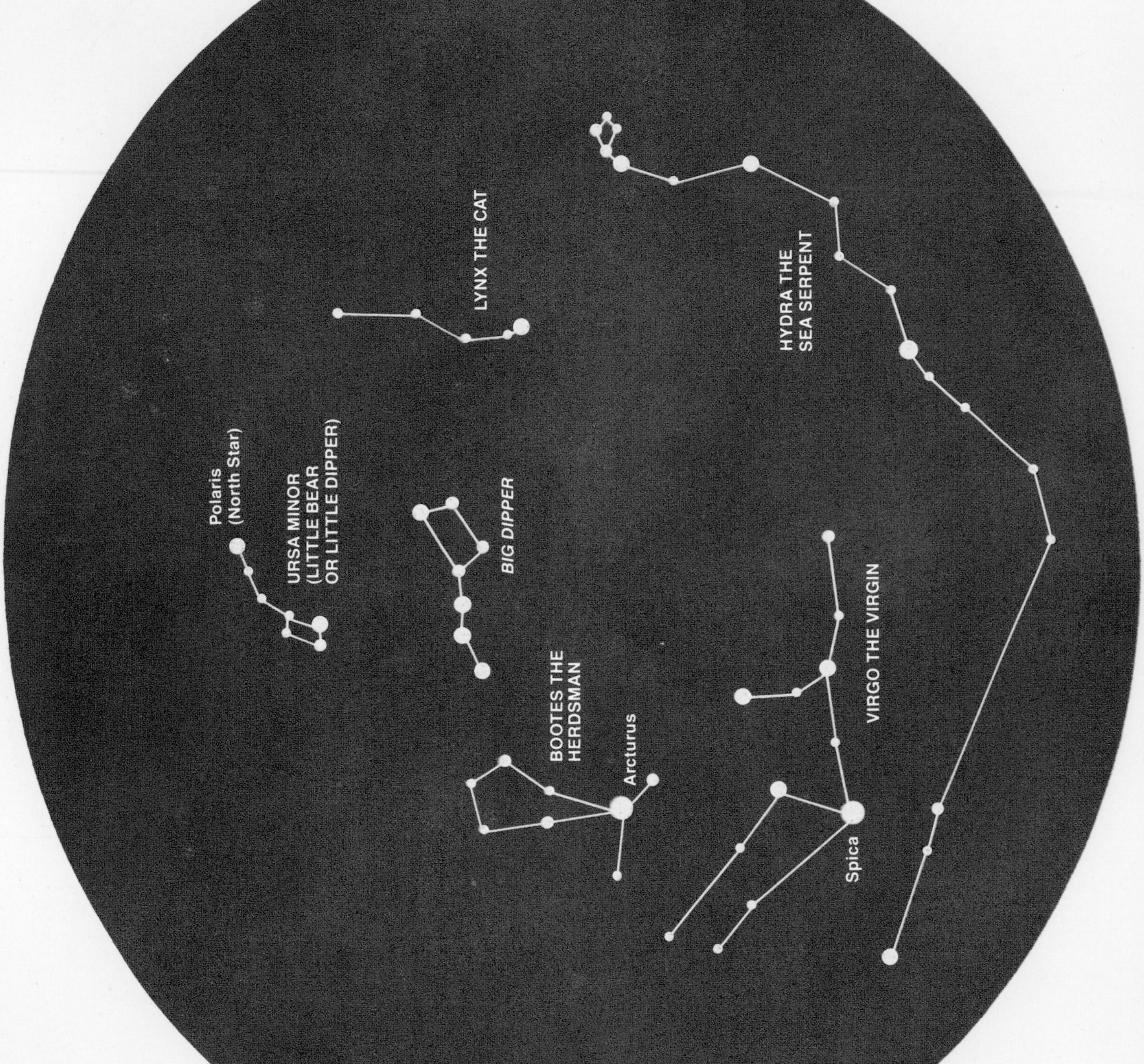

LYNX THE CAT

HYDRA THE
SEA SERPENT

Polaris
(North Star)

URSA MINOR
(LITTLE BEAR
OR LITTLE DIPPER)

BIG DIPPER

VIRGO THE VIRGIN

BOOTES THE
HERDSMAN

Arcturus

Spica

EARTH

Map shows the sky at:

11:00 P.M. on April 1
11:00 P.M. on April 15
10:00 P.M. on May 1
9:00 P.M. on May 15
8:00 P.M. on June 1

TOTAL ECLIPSE
OF THE SUN

MERCURY

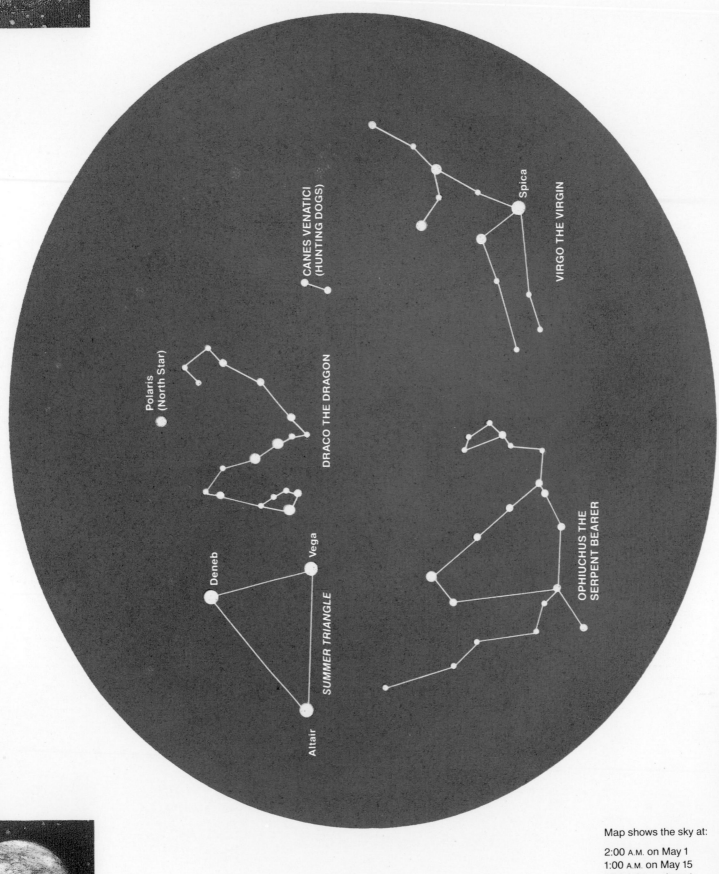

CANES VENATICI
(HUNTING DOGS)

Spica

VIRGO THE VIRGIN

Polaris
(North Star)

DRACO THE DRAGON

Vega

Deneb

OPHIUCHUS THE
SERPENT BEARER

SUMMER TRIANGLE

Altair

Map shows the sky at:

2:00 A.M. on May 1
1:00 A.M. on May 15
Midnight on June 1
11:00 P.M. on June 15
10:00 P.M. on July 1
9:00 P.M. on July 15

VENUS

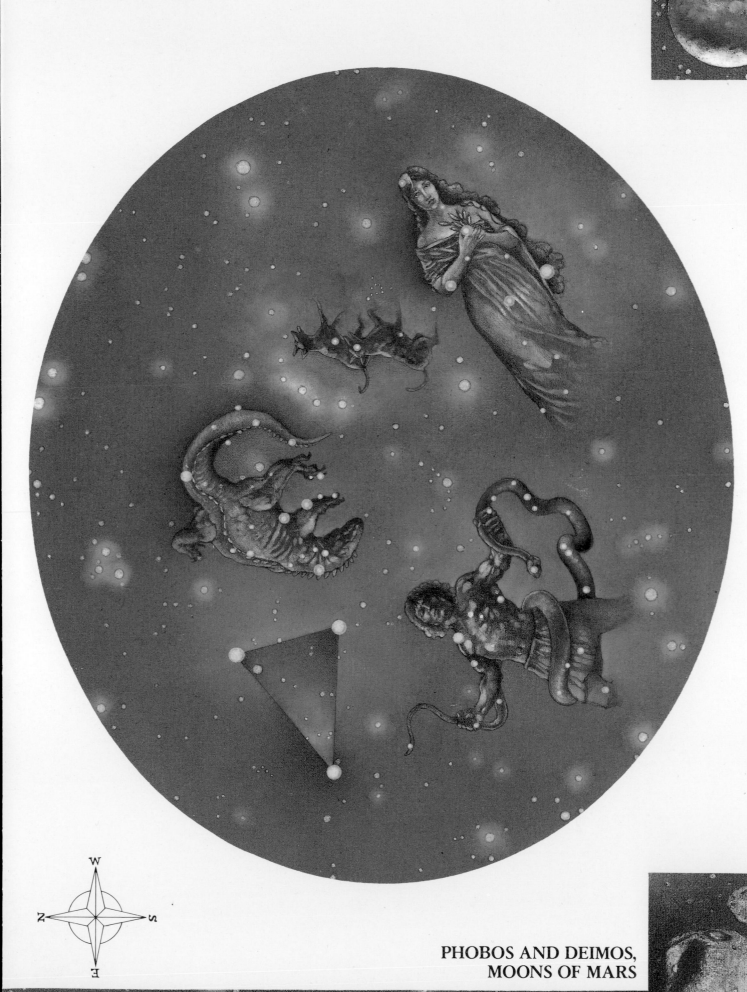

EARLY SUMMER

MARS

PHOBOS AND DEIMOS,
MOONS OF MARS

JUPITER

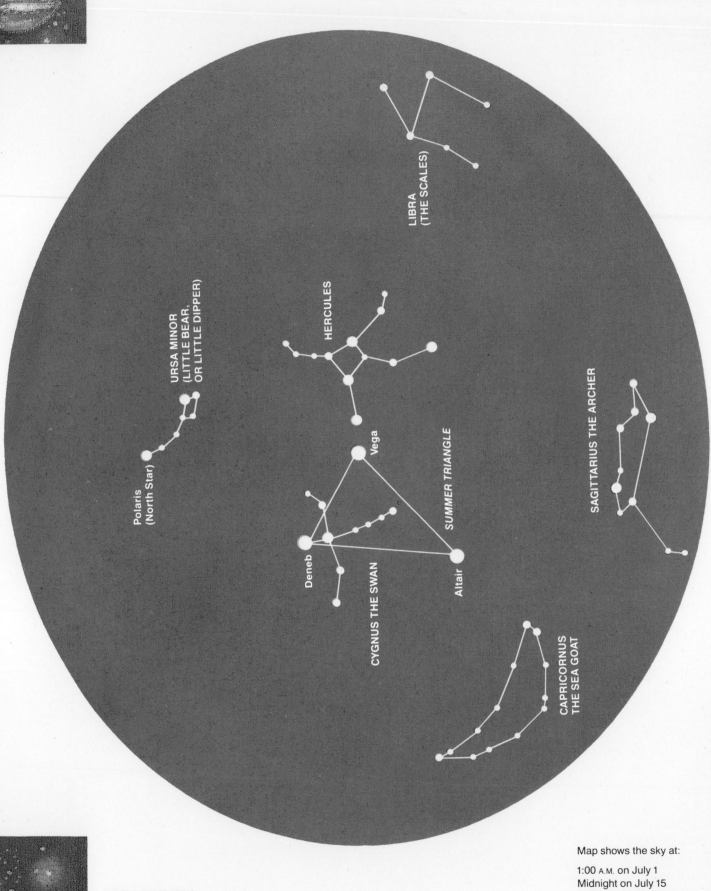

LIBRA (THE SCALES)

HERCULES

URSA MINOR (LITTLE BEAR, OR LITTLE DIPPER)

Polaris (North Star)

Vega

SUMMER TRIANGLE

SAGITTARIUS THE ARCHER

Deneb

Altair

CYGNUS THE SWAN

CAPRICORNUS THE SEA GOAT

AMALTHEA, ONE OF JUPITER'S SMALLEST MOONS

Map shows the sky at:

1:00 A.M. on July 1
Midnight on July 15
11:00 P.M. on August 1
10:00 P.M. on August 15
9:00 P.M. on September 1
8:00 P.M. on September 15

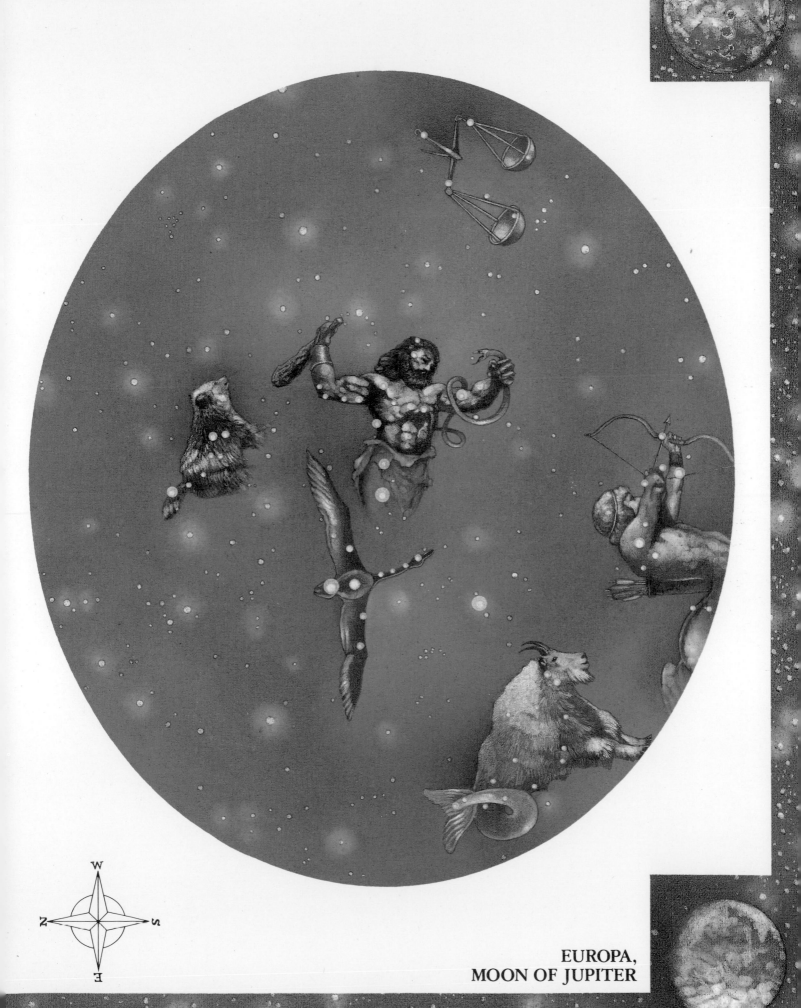

IO, MOON OF JUPITER

EUROPA,
MOON OF JUPITER

SATURN

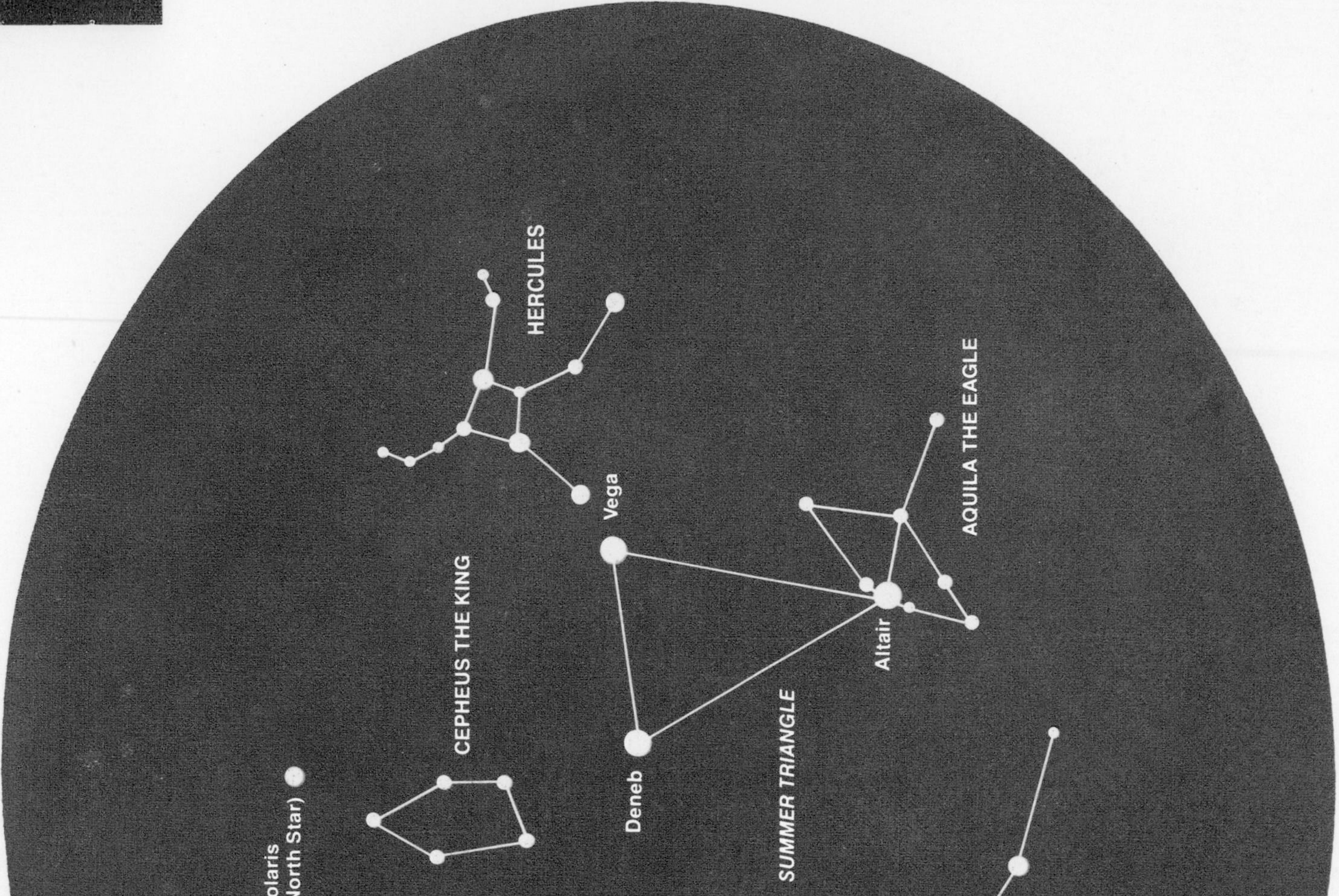

HERCULES

CEPHEUS THE KING

Vega

AQUILA THE EAGLE

Altair

SUMMER TRIANGLE

Deneb

Polaris
(North Star)

AQUARIUS THE
WATER CARRIER

ARIES THE RAM

ENCELADUS,
MOON OF SATURN

Map shows the sky at:

11:00 P.M. on September 1
10:00 P.M. on September 15
9:00 P.M. on October 1
8:00 P.M. on October 15
6:00 P.M. on November 1
5:00 P.M. on November 15

EARLY FALL

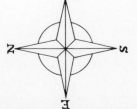

URANUS

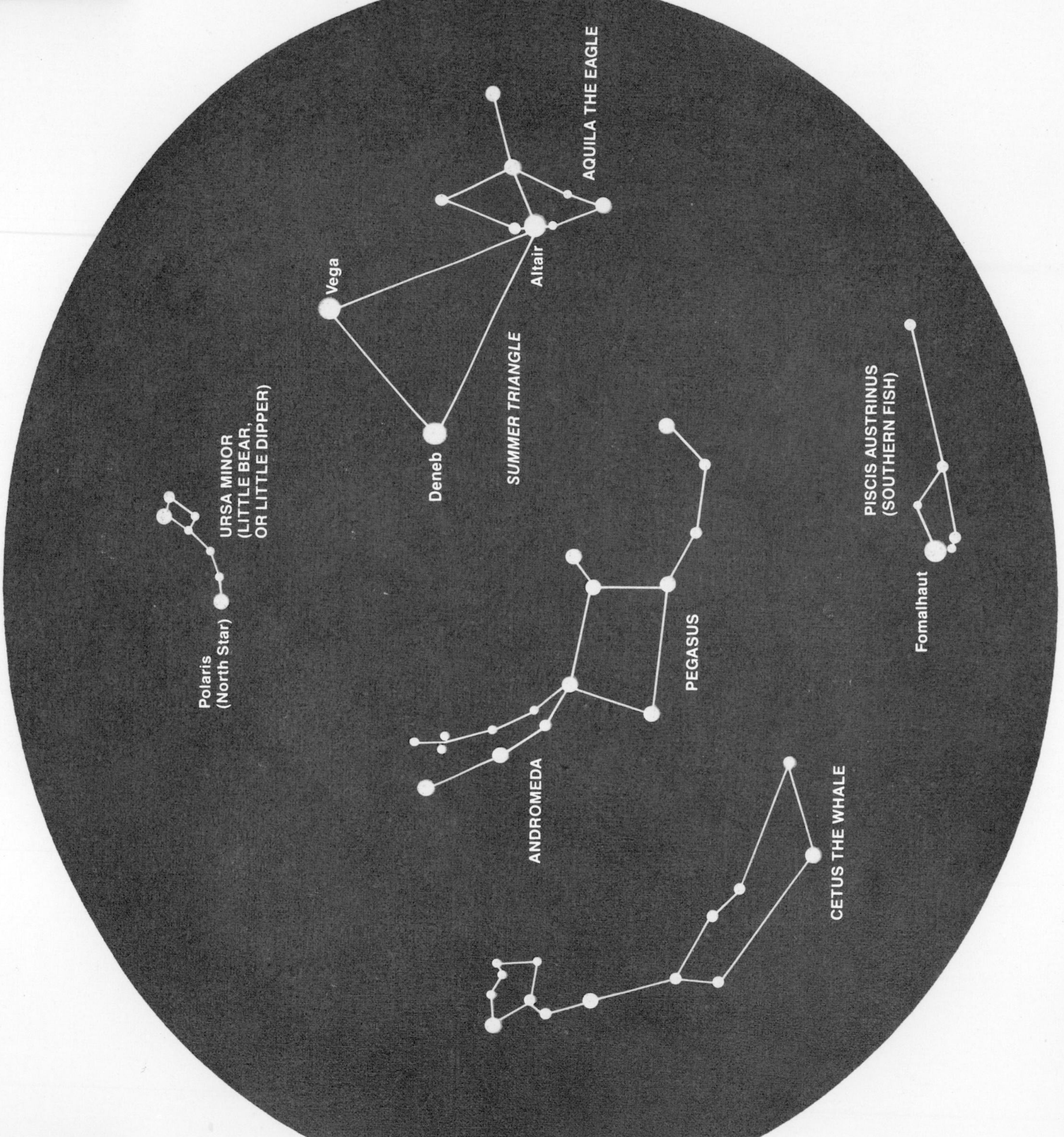

AQUILA THE EAGLE

Vega

Altair

SUMMER TRIANGLE

Deneb

URSA MINOR
(LITTLE BEAR,
OR LITTLE DIPPER)

Polaris
(North Star)

PISCIS AUSTRINUS
(SOUTHERN FISH)

Fomalhaut

PEGASUS

ANDROMEDA

CETUS THE WHALE

TITANIA,
MOON OF URANUS

Map shows the sky at:

11:30 P.M. on October 1
10:30 P.M. on October 15
8:30 P.M. on November 1
7:30 P.M. on November 15
6:30 P.M. on December 1

NEPTUNE

TRITON,
MOON OF NEPTUNE

PLUTO

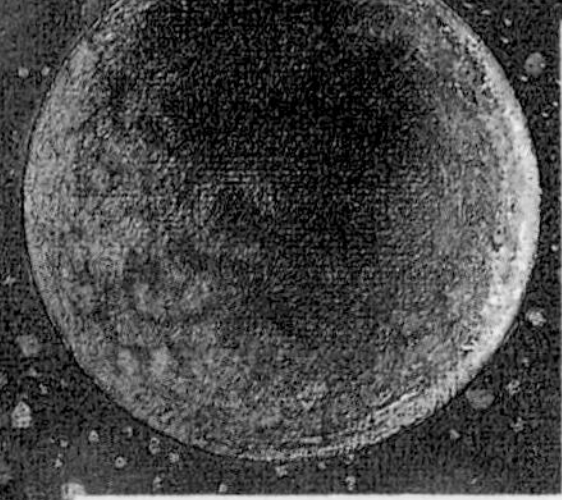

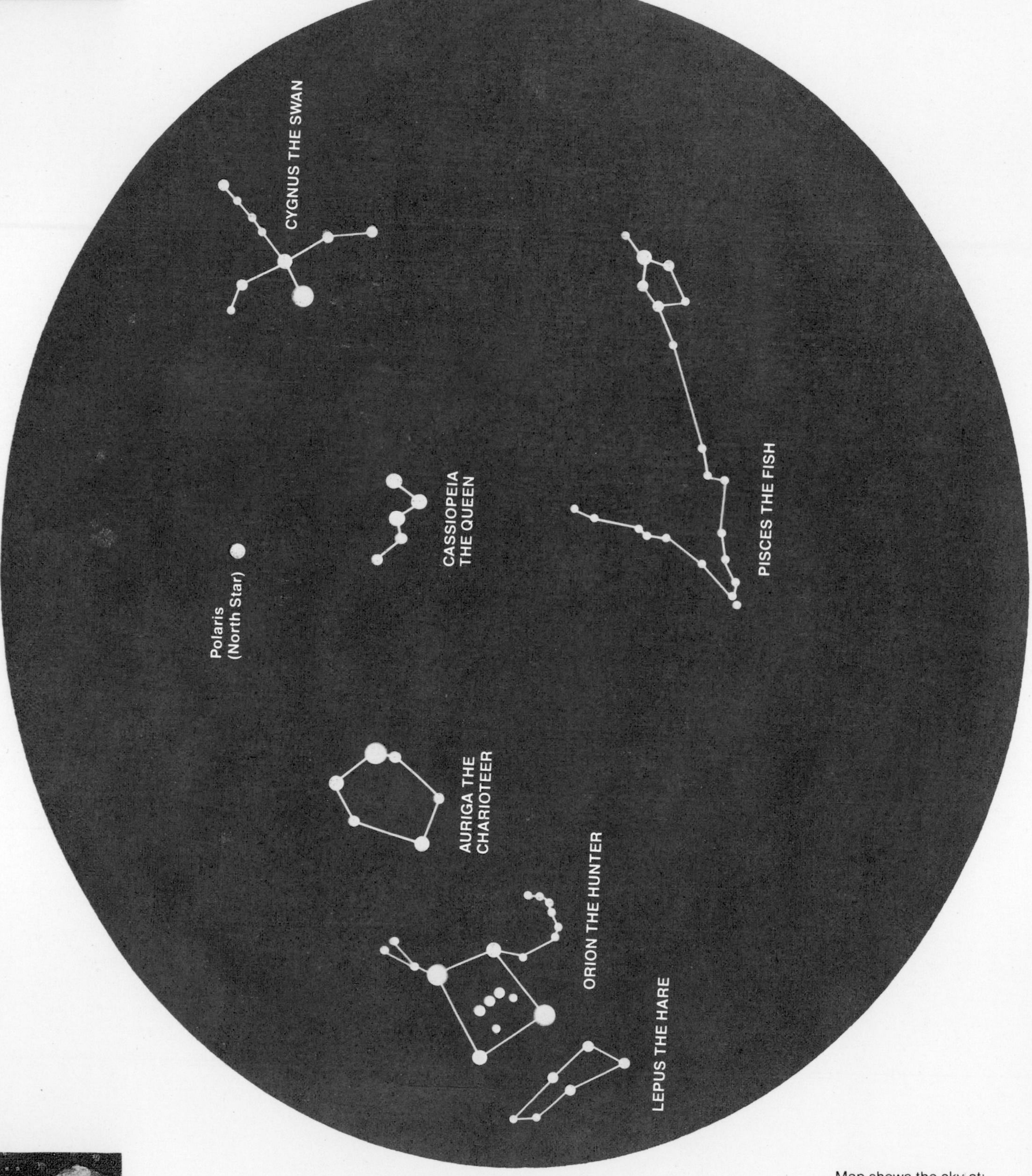

ASTEROIDS

CYGNUS THE SWAN

PISCES THE FISH

CASSIOPEIA
THE QUEEN

Polaris
(North Star)

AURIGA THE
CHARIOTEER

ORION THE HUNTER

LEPUS THE HARE

Map shows the sky at:

10:00 P.M. on November 15
9:00 P.M. on December 1
8:00 P.M. on December 15
7:00 P.M. on January 1
6:00 P.M. on January 15
5:00 P.M. on February 1

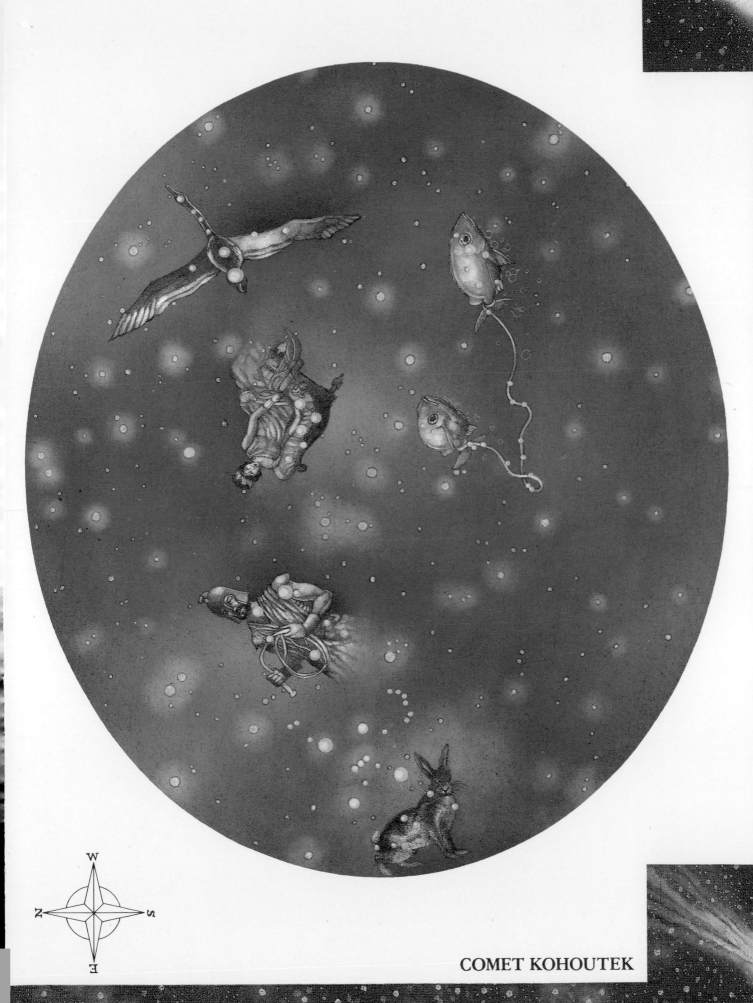

EARLY WINTER

HALLEY'S COMET

COMET KOHOUTEK

SPIRAL GALAXY

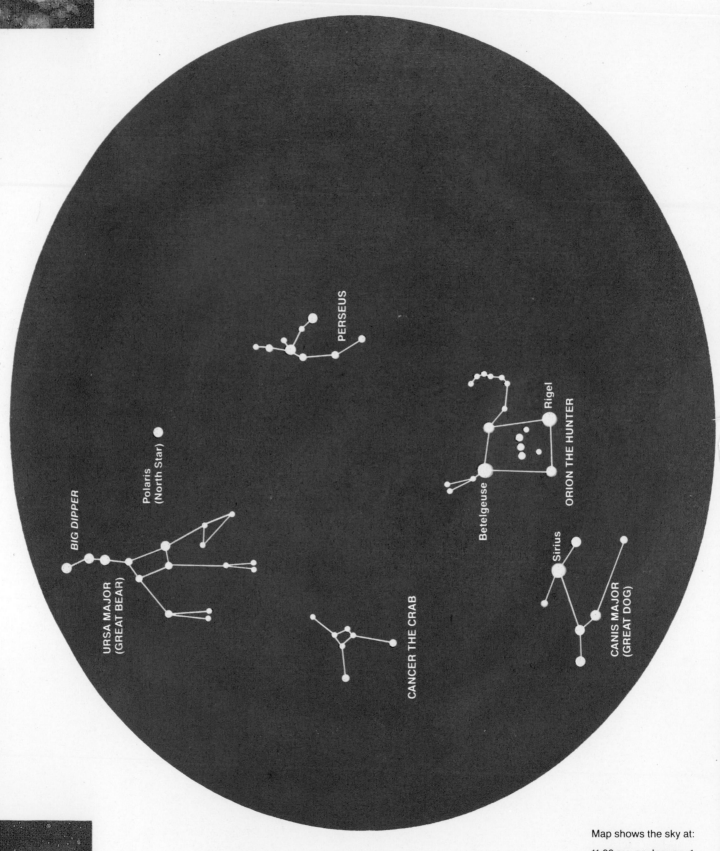

PERSEUS

Rigel

ORION THE HUNTER

Polaris
(North Star)

Betelgeuse

BIG DIPPER

Sirius

URSA MAJOR
(GREAT BEAR)

CANCER THE CRAB

CANIS MAJOR
(GREAT DOG)

Map shows the sky at:

11:00 P.M. on January 1
10:00 P.M. on January 15
9:00 P.M. on February 1
8:00 P.M. on February 15
7:00 P.M. on March 1
6:00 P.M. on March 15

ELLIPTICAL GALAXY

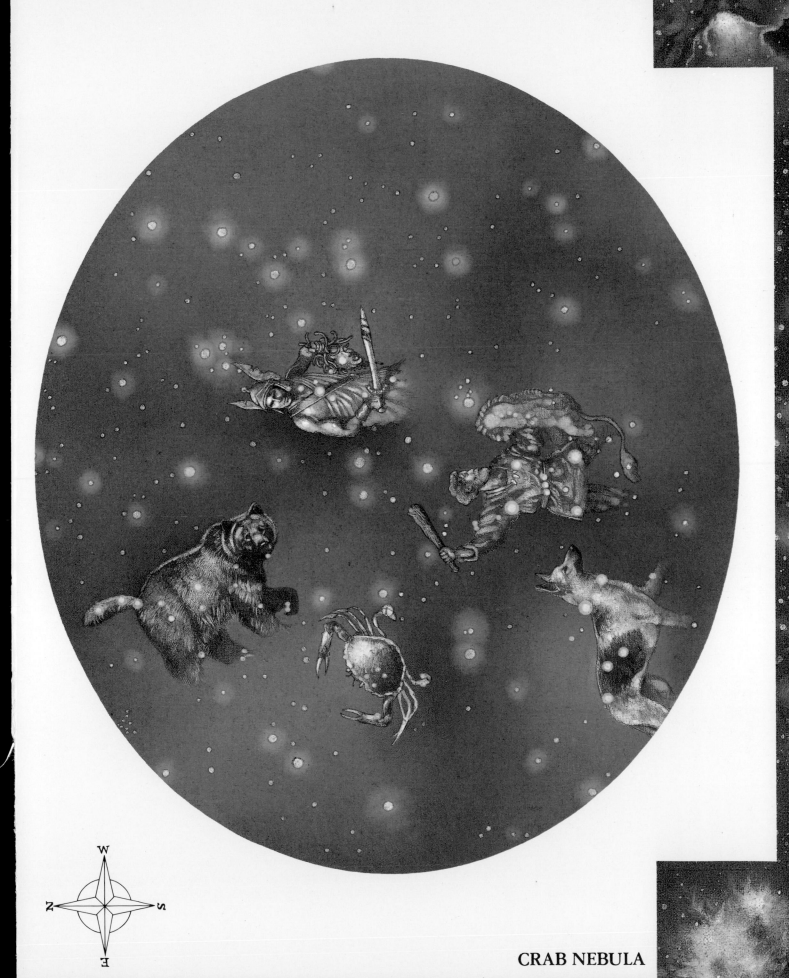

ABOUT THE CONSTELLATIONS

Andromeda. In Greek legends, Andromeda was the daughter of CASSIOPEIA and CEPHEUS. PERSEUS saved her from the sea monster CETUS.

Aquarius (the Water Carrier). The Babylonians saw this group of stars as a man pouring water from a jar.

Aquila (the Eagle). A companion of Jupiter, the king of the Roman gods.

Aries (the Ram). The golden fleece of this ram was the prize carried off by the Greek hero Jason, leader of the Argonauts.

Auriga (the Charioteer). A legendary king of Athens, Greece, who was said to have invented the chariot.

Boötes (the Herdsman). With his two dogs (CANES VENATICI), Boötes chases the Great Bear and the Little Bear (URSA MAJOR and URSA MINOR) around the sky.

Cancer (the Crab). A monster in Greek legends who attacked HERCULES while he was fighting the sea serpent HYDRA.

Canes Venatici (the Hunting Dogs). BOÖTES the herdsman's two dogs (see above).

Canis Major (the Great Dog). The faithful companion of ORION the hunter.

Capricornus (the Sea Goat). In the legends of many cultures, this creature, with the head of a goat and the tail of a fish, could travel on both land and sea.

Cassiopeia and **Cepheus.** The queen and king of Ethiopia; parents of ANDROMEDA. The main stars of Cassiopeia form a rough W shape.

Cetus (the Whale). The sea monster that nearly ate ANDROMEDA before she was rescued by PERSEUS. Cetus was turned to stone when Perseus flashed the head of Medusa at him.

Cygnus (the Swan). Greek legends say that Zeus, the king of the gods, sometimes disguised himself as a swan.

Draco (the Dragon). This constellation has been associated with many legendary monsters. One of them is a dragon killed by HERCULES.

Gemini (the Twins). The twins were Castor and Pollux, two devoted brothers in Greek legends.

Hercules. To the ancient Greeks, Hercules was the strongest and bravest man on earth. He killed many monsters, some of whom also became constellations (see CANCER, DRACO, HYDRA, and LEO).

Hydra (the Sea Serpent). A many-headed monster killed by HERCULES. Hydra is the largest constellation in the sky.

Leo (the Lion). The fiercest lion in the world.

No weapons would wound him. HERCULES solved that problem by choking the life out of him.

Lepus (the Hare). While being hunted by ORION, Lepus the hare slipped between his feet to hide.

Libra (the Scales). To the Romans, this group of stars represented the scales of justice.

Lynx (the Cat). This constellation was named Lynx because only those with eyes as keen as a lynx's will be able to find it.

Ophiuchus (the Serpent Bearer). Ancient people saw in this group of stars the shape of a man holding a huge snake.

Orion (the Hunter). The brightest and most easily recognized constellation in the winter sky. Orion was the companion of Artemis, Greek goddess of the hunt.

Pegasus. This is the winged horse that PERSEUS was riding when he saved ANDROMEDA from the sea monster CETUS.

Perseus. The Greek hero who, among other brave deeds, killed the monster Medusa. Medusa's face was so horrible that anyone who looked at her turned instantly to stone.

Pisces (the Fish). Pisces represents Venus, the Roman goddess of love and beauty, and her son Cupid. To escape from a monster, they turned into fish and jumped into a river.

Piscis Austrinus (the Southern Fish). A constellation with only one bright star. It is sometimes shown drinking water being poured by AQUARIUS.

Sagittarius (the Archer). This constellation is usually shown as a centaur—a creature that was half man, half horse—aiming his bow and arrow at a giant scorpion.

Summer Triangle. Not a constellation but a triangle made up of three bright stars from three different constellations: Vega (in Lyra, the Lyre), Altair (in AQUILA), and Deneb (in CYGNUS).

Taurus (the Bull). In Greek myth, Zeus disguised himself as a snow-white bull in order to win the heart of a princess.

Ursa Major (the Great Bear). When Zeus fell in love with Callisto, his jealous wife changed Callisto into a bear. Ursa Major includes the Big Dipper, the best-known group of stars in the sky.

Ursa Minor (the Little Bear). Callisto and Zeus had a son, whom Zeus changed into a bear and put in the sky. Ursa Minor is also called the Little Dipper. It includes Polaris, the North Star.

Virgo (the Virgin). The Greek goddess of justice. This constellation has also been associated with Ceres, goddess of the harvest.